MINDSET SKILLSET

Success Secrets for Unlimited Growth

By

Steve Owbridge

ISBN: 9798764523910

Contact the Author at mindsetskillset@owbridge.com

www.owbridge.com

CONTENTS

ACKNOWLEDGMENTS

I would like to thank my life and business partner Isabel. She is the rock of our family and her love, care, dedication to us and our family is mind blowing. We have taken an incredible journey and are living an awesome adventure together. This book would not have made it without her.

Our three boys Kevin, Nicholas and Micah for their inspiration and teaching me patience. It has been a joy to see them all grow as I've shared the contents of this book at our many family dinner discussions. I am so proud of the young men they are growing into.

My parents, Alan & Jan, for always believing in me and telling me my whole life that I can do anything I want to. Jan has been an incredible support in the process of writing this book, correcting my grammar and spelling, often, and helping me to verbalise some of the massive amounts of information I have in my head.

My little sister, (only 4 years younger) Kelly, for looking up to me and reminding me to be the best example I can be. Little sisters are always watching big brothers!

My leaders, my team and colleagues in my business who are a constant inspiration to keep going and become the best leader I can be.

My brother, Frank Eguridu who is, as my mum calls him, "The kindest man she has ever met". He has been the alternative opinion, encourager and my buddy for over a decade.

Jeff Lestz, CEO, Genistar Ltd for his belief in me and his example of courage, humility and integrity and for his leap of faith in starting our company.

There are a countless number of unnamed people who have inspired me over the last 50 years. I appreciate them all.

Thank you.

DISCLAIMER

Applying the principles in this book can change your life forever. If you are happy with where you are and don't want to grow, please do not read any further.

INTRODUCTION

Are you struggling to succeed in life or business? Do you seem to keep trying and trying and yet the results don't change? Are you fed up trying to achieve goals and failing? Are you ready to change all that?

What would your life look like if you could learn how to harness the combined power of mastering your subconscious mind alongside learning and applying practical business and life skills?

In this book I share proven and practical lessons I've learned through several successful careers and businesses over several decades. It is a manual, a workbook, a storybook and a journal. Whether it's how to programme your subconscious mind for success, how to choose a business or how to make smarter financial decisions, this book is for you.

I encourage you to read it with a pen or pencil in hand. Make notes, scribble in the margins, complete the exercises and highlight the nuggets, of which there are many. This book has been described as a one stop shop for success. You will definitely want to read it more than once!

By engaging in this learning and inspirational development process, you will gain valuable insight into yourself, your business or job and your life and be equipped to make changes.

There are two reasons why I started writing a book. I've be told for many years "Steve, write a book so then you can position yourself as an author". I was told that it doesn't even need to be that good as it's more of a 'big business card'. This never sat well with me. I always thought that if I was going to take the time to write a book, I wanted it to make an impact. I want it to outlive me and leave a legacy.

As a parent, I also want to leave a legacy for my children, grandchildren, great grandchildren and beyond. I thought, "what would I want teach them about life, business, success and mindset if I were to live another 100 years?" This book is a result of me answering that question and wanting to impact your life, too, as well as generations to come.

When I started to write, I had been doing lots of seminars called 'Change Your Financial Life'. They are only about 90 minutes long and always make a great impact. In spite of their success I always felt that there was only so much I could fit into an hour and a half and yet there was so much more to teach.

I decided to write a book of the same title. However, as I wrote and began exploring the deepest content in more depth, I became aware that this was not just a book about changing your financial life but your life in general, your mindset, your understanding of existing concepts, so I had to come up with a new title.

Some of the working titles have been:

Change Your Financial Life

Change Your Life

The Real Secret

The Law of ACTION

The YOU-Niverse

The Law of Attraction The Law of You

MasterMindset

And many more…

I settled on the current title as I think it encompasses the essence of what I am trying to convey. How you have the power to change your mindset and upskill to change your life, in reality not just in theory.

Please read and share the contents of this book with anyone you feel will benefit. I would love to hear your success stories and what inspired you the most.

Feel free to email me at mindsetskillset@owbridge.com

CHAPTER ONE

THE SECRET

Millions of people have read the best-selling book 'The Secret' over the years and there is an ever-growing culture of trainers and coaches teaching that you can 'speak to the universe' and talk things into being, through the law of attraction, and they will be manifested. Vibrating at a higher frequency, through being grateful and positive as well as affirmations and visualisations and speaking to the Universe - ASK, BELIEVE, RECEIVE. Ask the Universe for anything you want, define it clearly (I will share more on having a clear concise mental picture later) then believe that the Universe will give you your desires.

You can do this through visualisation, vision boards, gratitude and giving from abundance and then receive, act as though you have what you want already until it manifests. When you vibrate at a higher frequency you attract the things that you have asked for. There is nothing wrong with this perspective, and if it is working for you, then change nothing.

Another perspective is that we use a tiny fraction of our brains' incredible capacity and that the way we think is a result of the programming we have received up to this point in our lives, from parents, siblings, and our social environment.

Imagining the brain as a bio-computer, as author Ron G Holland calls it, in his book 'Turbo Success' (which I highly recommend) and at the time of writing this you can get the pdf version for free on Ron's website.

Ron shares that the left and right sides of our brain handle different things. The left is all about logic, intellect and words and the right is creative, imaginative, images and so on. We have a part of the brain called a Reticular Activating System or 'RAS', which filters out unnecessary information. It's like a door or gatekeeper to our subconscious mind.

For example, if someone lives near an airport, directly under the flight path, very quickly the RAS filters out the noise of the planes flying overhead as they are not relevant but are very noticeable to visitors who are not used to hearing them. We are programmed with thoughts and behaviours from birth and the type of programming we have received has a direct impact on how we act, and even progress in life, business, relationships and pretty much everything else.

The good news is that we can reprogramme our mindset through unlocking the RAS, and replacing old or wrong 'programmes' with new ones. This means that we can reprogramme our mindset to become more tuned in to the things we want.

For example, have you ever wanted a new car? You thought about it, dreamed about it, watched videos, read the brochures maybe even visited a showroom and had a test drive. You have inserted that car into your conscious mind and now you start to notice those types of car everywhere. It's as if by putting that car into your conscious mind, your subconscious has become tuned in to that type of car then your subconscious goes to work on solving the problem of getting you the car.

Your subconscious goes to work on solving problems that you give it to solve. If you don't give it anything to work on, then it doesn't. It's like it's on standby, awaiting more instructions. There is much more to explain on both of these perspectives which I won't cover in too much detail in this book. But what I want you to consider is this:

The way I look at both teachings is this: the first is an external locus of control, which means that you are looking to external forces to solve problems or make provision - from God, the Universe or the Source, as it's sometimes called. Following steps to allow the power of the universe to work and attract wealth, happiness, etc. to you. Yes, there are internal things you need to do to 'plug in', but ultimately, it's about resonating at a higher frequency to attract.

The second perspective is an internal locus of control, taking responsibility for how you think. The data or instructions you insert into your subconscious mind to work on problem solving which, by the way, can also mean becoming more tuned in to opportunities, people, and lead to greater wealth and success.

What if both perspectives are true and, by adopting both, you can find out what yields you the best results? They are not in conflict and, in fact, have many similarities. Even people who teach the Law of Attraction and The Secret, learn skills to promote their training, YouTube channels, books, seminars etc.. they do not just manifest by asking, believing and receiving. ACTION is also required in the law of AttrACTION! This book shares some practical action steps to help you on your journey to success. Every chapter is filled with wisdom nuggets that, if you apply them, can have a profound impact on your life.

ACTION IS ALSO REQUIRED IN THE LAW OF ATTR-ACTION!

Some of these trainers, coaches, gurus and experts are genuine people, with good intentions while others are charlatan scam artists. I will leave it with you to make your own mind up on who is who.

Many people teach this because they believe it and some because they know it's just what people want to believe, and it makes them a good living by teaching it.

It's the ideal product! If it's not working for you, then it's not the course, the coach or the book's fault - it's you that must be doing something wrong, right? As someone once told me, the key to being successful in business is simple, *"find out what people want and give it to them or show them how to get it."* I agree with this too, however there are many people who have been believing, trusting, speaking out affirmations and so on, who have not seen the results they crave. Or maybe it seems to work sometimes, but not others. Maybe you can relate to this?

Now, I am not saying that The Secret and the Law of Attraction are wrong. I practice some of things they teach, too. Whether you choose to call it the law of attraction, God, the Universe or something else, in my experience, there is a universal power that is at work to help people achieve success that you can tap into.

What if you could do practical things to enhance this universal power? Would you be willing to learn them? What if some of the things many people attribute to God or the Universe are sometimes a result of learned skills, strategies and a mindset that is applied habitually?

Wouldn't it be useful to learn those skills too and add to your belief, and increase your chances of success?

I believe that true success is composed of many things from having a balanced life, providing for your family or just living your best life, but it is achieved not only through belief and talking to God or the Universe and not just the law of attraction, but also by learning skills and strategies that you can apply too.

In this book I share many systems, strategies, skills and exercises to help you on your journey to changing your life and achieving success in finance, business and life in general. As the well-known bible verse states 'Faith without works is dead'.

Instead of just asking the Universe or just trying to achieve your goals based on what you know and how you think now, why not combine the power of God, the Universe or Source and develop YOUr mindset and skillset and build, using the power of the YOU-NIVERSE.

CHAPTER TWO

THE END

“I wish I had loads of money”, my son, Micah, told me.

“Why? I asked.

“I just want to be rich” he said, with excitement in his eyes.

“But, why do you want to have lots of money?” I asked him again.

Confused, the boy said, “to buy nice things and have a nice life of course”.

“What things, Micah?” I inquired.

“I don’t know, just toys, sweets, gadgets and stuff.”

“Yes Micah, but what, specifically, do you want to buy?” I pressed him again.

“I don’t know Dad, just nice things!”

I asked him how much money he has saved right now.

“Not much!” he said, looking down at the floor, then lifting his head and with a cheeky grin, he exclaimed, “that’s why I need more!”

“Before you can get money to get what you want, Micah, you need to know ‘what’ you want. You need to be specific, do your research and find out how much the things cost. Decide when you want. Then, and only then, can you really figure out how to get the money you need to buy them.
You need to know how much money you have right now, how much you will need and when you want to buy the things you want.”

“How can someone plot a journey to a destination if they don’t know where they are going? Does that make sense?” he asked Micah.

“It makes sense, Dad. So, I need to decide what I want first, then see what I have now and then work out how to get it, right?”

I looked down at Micah, “Exactly!” I said.

“It sounds simple” Micah said.

I smiled at him and said, "It is simple, it's just not always easy but if you do the right thing and follow the steps it becomes a lot easier."

Everyone wants to have an amazing life, financial freedom, time freedom and the power of choice. The problem is that most people never take the time to learn the fundamentals of how to be financially successful. Financial success doesn't necessarily mean wealthy - for everyone it's different. You need to decide for yourself what it means to you - whatever income or net worth you decide is financial freedom for you. If you're not there yet, you need to assess where you are now. As the saying goes 'even the longest journey starts with a single step'.

In this book, I will share some techniques and strategies to help you on your financial journey as well as challenge you with some exercises to complete to give you some clarity and direction. My goal is that, by the time you finish this book, you will know where you are, where you want to be and how to get there. Feel free to write notes, fill in the blanks and scribble in the margins. By the way, if you don't take action, from what you learn here, it doesn't work!

Exercise: A SNAPSHOT OF YOUR CURRENT FINANCIAL LIFE

I want you write down three figures:

Write Down How much Income you take home every month after tax and and deductions. What actually goes into your bank account? £1,000, £1,500, £2,000?

Write down how much unsecured debt you have, things like credit cards, loans, overdrafts etc. Add them up and put the total.

Write down how much total savings or investments you have. For many people this is very low or even zero. If it's £0 for you, still write it down. e.g.

CURRENT YOU (example)

Income	£1,500	£ ______________
Debt	£20,000	£ ______________
Savings	£1,000	£ ______________

Now, ask yourself, when you look at these figures, how does it make you feel knowing that this is where you are now? How satisfied are you?

Write down three words that describe how you feel or the emotions you have when confronted with these figures?

How Do you Feel about Your Current Situation?

1____

2____

3____

If you are being really honest with yourself these are typically negative words such as frustrated, sad, annoyed, depressed or even, hopeless. That's fine. It's important to acknowledge your present reality before you start to build a new one.

Just like Micah, in the story, you need to recognise where you are, what you have and that you're at the beginning of your journey; then you can work out what you want to be different.

Now you know where you are, you can start to work out where you want to be.

That's the next step!

Imagine you could be magically transported to 12 months from today! What would you want those figures to be? How much would you like your income to be? Be stretchingly realistic at this point. If you earn £1,500 a month right now, to start making £50,000 a month is unlikely in just 12 months, for most people. One of the keys to becoming an habitual goal achiever is to set stretchingly realistic goals, not unrealistic ones. We will cover this in more detail later in this book.

Write down three more figures. These are the amounts that you would like the current figures to become in the next 12 months. Perhaps another £2,000 income per month would make a big impact. For most families even an extra £1,000 more income per month would have a massive impact for their families.

Maybe you would like to be debt free? If this is the case put £0. But if you have a really large amount of debt you can put what you would like it to come down to in the next 12 months.

Finally, how much would you want to have in your savings? Enough for a deposit for a house, a holiday, an emergency fund etc.? Write that down too.

FUTURE YOU (OR 12 MONTH YOU) Example

Using the following as an example, enter the figures you would like in 12 months

Income e.g. £3,000 £ ________________

Debt e.g. £0 £ ________________

Savings e.g.£15,000 £ ________________

As before, based on the figures you have entered above, write down three words to describe how you would feel if it was 12 months from today - if you were taking home that income, have that level of debt or none at all and have that amount in your savings.

Which words best describe the feeling?

1.______________________________________

2. ______________________________________

3. ______________________________________

If you have done this correctly, these words are usually positive ones like, happy, ecstatic, relieved, awesome, or even freedom!

So, now you have identified where you are financially and where you want to be in 12 months. Now, you just have to figure out how to make this happen!

CHAPTER THREE

FUTURE YOU

"So Micah, what toy or gadget do you really want the most?" I asked Micah.

"Hmm, if I had to choose just one I think it would definitely be a bike."

"That's good. What type of bike?"

"Ummm, a red one!" he said, now getting excited about the prospect of getting a bike.

"That's good that you know the colour, son, but there are thousands of different types of bikes and many of them are red. You need to be more specific - decide not only on the colour but the type of bike you want.

“For example, is it a racing bike? a mountain bike? a BMX bike? It’s important to get really specific with your goals.”

“OK Dad, I want a red mountain bike!”

“Great! What size? Which features? What will it be made of? How much will it cost?”

“Hmm, I think I need to find out more about the bike before I can figure out how to get it Dad.”

“That’s the start of the journey, Son.”

With that, Micah went off to ‘Google’ mountain bikes!

Setting and achieving goals is a system. It’s a skill that you can learn to master and you can make hitting your goals a habit.

As with anything, it just needs to be learned and practiced. This means that anyone can do it, including you!

Learn it. Practice it. Form the habit.

There are many perspectives on how to achieve your goals. Some are great and proven but you must find a system that works for you. For me, something that has always worked is recognising that goal achieving consists of three parts that all interlock, like cogs in a machine.

Imagine a simple machine with three cogs. One larger than the other 2 and on one of the others a handle.

COG ONE - CCMP

The first cog is the goal or, as Andrew Carnegie calls it, a "Clear Concise Mental Picture" (CCMP) or a "Definiteness of Purpose" Goals must be specific and detailed. Many people have taught about S.M.A.R.T goals that must be Specific, Measurable, Achievable, Realistic and with a Time Frame and that's absolutely correct but, it's only part of the process. This is the 'What' Cog.

I remember asking a young lady what her goals were, and she told me that her goal was to build an orphanage.
"That's a great goal" I said, "Where are you going to build it"

"Hmm, Africa somewhere." She replied.

"You know, Africa is a really big place. Maybe you should narrow it down to a country or even a city, at least", I said.

I then asked her a few more questions about this orphanage. "How many kids will it be for? How much will it cost? When do you want to have it built by?" I challenged her.

“Hmm, I’m not sure”, she mused.

I told her that, whilst this was a great goal and it was good that she wanted to help people, if she didn’t get more specific about it then it would just be a pipe dream that makes her feel good about herself but would never get anything achieved.

It is essential to drill down and get the details on your goal.

Imagine that you had a blank cheque to get your goal or, in her case, to build the orphanage now. What would you need to know? How would you spend it? And yes, I know that all goals are not based on money, but money can usually help with most of them.

Someone once told me that they were not money motivated, and they were all about developing themselves spiritually. I asked what they would need to do be able to devote more time to this personal journey. I asked her what was stopping her from making more progress.

She replied that they would need to leave their job and attend more retreats. I asked if the retreats were free and if she had enough money saved so she could stop working for her employer. She told me that the retreats were actually quite expensive as they were abroad and she couldn’t go on as many as she would like to as she didn’t have that much holiday time left from her employer.

“So, would money help?” I asked.

She conceded that it would. Money is not the goal it’s the tool that gives you the power to choose how you spend your time.

MONEY IS NOT THE GOAL, IT'S THE TOOL THAT GIVES YOU THE POWER TO CHOOSE HOW YOU SPEND YOUR TIME

The great thing, in the age in which we live, is that it's easy to research our goals using the internet. Google, Pinterest, YouTube etc., all give us insights into everything from pictures of the water bungalow we would love to visit in the Maldives, the car we would like to own reviewed by experts, professional images we can take inspiration from on our vision boards and screen wallpapers etc.

Research your goals now as if you were going to achieve them now. Having a clear concise mental picture is the start of the process. As Andrew Carnegie states in the book 'Think and Grow Rich', "the first step from poverty to riches is the most difficult..." So, if it's the most difficult that suggests that you need to spend some time on it, researching, using your imagination, planning etc.

He also states that 'all riches and all material things that anyone acquires through self effort begins in the form of a Clear Concise Mental Picture of the thing one seeks."

IF YOU KNOW WHAT YOU WANT IT'S HARD TO ACHIEVE. IF YOU DON'T, IT'S IMPOSSIBLE

So, how do you get started? Start by asking yourself some questions and using your imagination.
If money was no object…

Get a notepad and treat this as an exercise to begin to plan the rest of your life. Write down the answers to the following questions. I've given some examples to work from but use your imagination! Be as creative and bold as you like – after all, it's YOUR dream. It's better to start big and work backwards than to aim low for something you don't really want.

As the saying goes, 'it's better to aim for the stars and hit the moon than to aim at the moon and miss'.

IT'S BETTER TO AIM FOR THE STARS AND HIT THE MOON

What do you want out of life?

Time freedom: the ability to do what you want, when you want, how you want, for the rest of your life.

To spend more time with your family and friends.

Just doing the things you love or are passionate about.

Perhaps it's financial freedom you need – to be able to buy or go anywhere you want without having financial constraints

What do you like to do?

What are your hobbies? Fishing, travel, going to concerts or shows, watching football – going to live sporting events whenever you choose. Maybe relaxing on a beach with white sand, the sun on your face, a turquoise ocean, and a cocktail in hand.

Helping people; supporting your local church or charity – an orphanage, a dog's home, or your children's school. Maybe, it's more about you. Are you passionate about sports cars, painting or pottery?

How would you like to spend your time?

Perhaps it's one of the hobbies you listed. Spending time with your grandkids? Outings with your children? Or something simple like reading a book, relaxing on a hammock, in your garden.

Your time is a limited resource. Every minute wasted on things that take you away from your goals or do not add value to your life, or the lives of others, are bad investments.

Treat every minute, hour, day, week, month, and year as precious. Once they have gone, they can't be recovered.

We always invest, save, spend, or waste time. Ask yourself which of these do you do and with how much of your time.

Who would you like to help?

Your partner, parents, children, your church, or charity. Maybe your friends – or even strangers!

How many times have you seen an advert come on TV, with images of starving children, with swollen bellies; or there has been a natural disaster of epic proportions – a volcano erupted, maybe floods or earthquakes that have devastated towns and communities?

The one thing they all have in common is that they are asking for help – usually in the form of money.

Money is the answer to most problems. If not, it can usually help. Money is influence and power to affect change. The more you have the more you can give and greater the impact you can make

What would you like to learn?

A new skill, like desktop publishing, knitting, or learning a new language. Or, perhaps you just want to commit more time to your own personal, spiritual, or physical growth through study, retreats or workshops etc.

As humans, we are designed to consistently grow. We have an inherent and unrivalled capacity for learning. It's been widely published and believed that we only use 10% of our brains. This is, in fact, a myth. However, we still only utilise a relatively small percentage of our brain's ability in comparison to its capacity.

Where would you like to live, or travel to?

In the country? By the sea? In a different country? In a warm country where you can bask in the sun or where

you can ski every day? Maybe you love where you live now but would like a bigger house or a nicer garden.

Visiting other countries and cultures

Some of the most common goals that people share with me when I coach and mentor them, are things like cruises, dream holidays, adventures that simply don't feel are realistic or possible for them.

You may also feel like your goals are impossible. I want to tell you that they are not! You have to believe it before you can achieve it. Achieving your goals, travel or otherwise, begin in your mind.

I will share with you how to programme your mindset and develop your faith in your ability to achieve your goals, later in this book.

What are you passionate about?

What causes, issues, politics, projects, or people inspire you? What do you, or would you do, if you don't, or didn't, get paid for it?

Most footballers play for the love of the game. The excitement of scoring a goal, making a save or winning a game; they thrive on being a part of a team, working towards a common goal.
Most of them played football before they were paid for it and will continue to play long after they stop being paid. When they can play no more, they will miss – and reminisce – over the thing that gave them so much joy.

If you can find the thing that makes you feel like this – and get paid for it – as the saying goes, you will never work another day in your life.

If you can't, then find the thing that makes you the money to give you the freedom to do the things that excite you and give you most joy.

What excites you?

As in the example above, perhaps for you, it's football!

Some people are excited about cruises. For example, my parents love to cruise. My Dad starts booking their next cruise before the latest one has even left port. He is passionate, as a Yorkshireman who likes to save money, about finding the best deals available. As he always says, "I'm a Yorkshireman. We have short arms and long pockets".

Mum gets excited about cruising, but it doesn't stop there. She is passionate about sharing what she loves about cruising, with others. She does this through 'Facebook Lives' from the ships and ports and she also create videos, which she shares on her YouTube channel – www.youtube.com/c/cruisequeen

What or who would you like to invest in?

Investment funds? Property? Land? Businesses? People?

Often when I speak to people about their goals, they tell me they would like to build a property portfolio, invest in stocks or businesses, etc. I usually ask why. Most of the time it transpires that the property portfolio or investment is, in fact, a vehicle to enable them to achieve their actual personal goal of freedom.

Some people ARE passionate about property and there are many courses, books, and seminars – some good, some great and some not – about this topic. I will leave this to the property professionals.

The key thing is to be able to identify of what you invest in is your passion or a pathway *to* your passion.

Investing in people, perhaps financially, by investing in a business idea or a training course for them or, in a non-financial way, such as coaching and mentoring, can be very rewarding.

One of the things that fires me up every day is my mission to help people to reach their goals, in reality, rather than just in theory. I take immense pride when one of my team or someone I have coached or mentored achieves their goals.

Each goal achieved motivates me to want to find others that I can equip and empower, with my knowledge and experience, to achieve their goals.

What car would you like to drive?

A BMW? Mercedes? Tesla? Rolls Royce? A Classic car or just a better car than you have now?

Whichever car you choose, it's important to know about it. One of the things I always tell people, is that they must become an expert in the thing they desire. This means getting specific about what you want. It's only then that you can work out how to get it.

What does financial freedom mean to you?

Not having to work. Having more money than you need? Having no debt? Being mortgage free?

Financial freedom is often defined as working because you want to, not because you *have* to. In reality, it is different for everyone. For some, £1500 a month passive income would give them the lifestyle they desire; for others it may be £50,000 a month.

Some people teach that you can work out your financial independence number using a formula. For example, the 'FIRE' movement (Financial Independence, Retire Early) focus on living below your means and putting all you can into an investment or retirement fund to get there as fast as possible. This works for many people.

Others focus on increasing income or finding additional revenue streams so they can maintain their lifestyle and still work towards an early retirement.
Whichever you choose, you need to commit to it. They both take planning, commitment, and discipline.

Some of these are not easy questions to answer quickly, or off the cuff; they take some serious thought and time. It is really important to spend time on this as it solidifies your purpose, in your mind.

If you are in a relationship, it's also a good idea to do these both individually and as a couple. You would be surprised at how many goals your partner has that they haven't shared with you yet. It's also good to do this with your kids.

One of things we do every year is have a family meeting with our 3 boys to discuss each of our personal goals and family goals. We each create a mind map of our goals and follow the '8Fs of a Balanced Life' model that I cover in a later chapter.

Once you have taken the time to decide what you actually want, and have really clarified these goals specifically, you must write them down. Committing them to paper forces you to be specific. It also solidifies them in your mind, as you have had to take a physical step towards them.

It's a good idea to not only write them as a list but also as a paragraph that you can read as an affirmation. You could write something like this, for example:

> *"I am confident. I am open minded. I am going to travel to the Maldives and stay in a water bungalow and own a blue BMW 4 Series Coupe within the next 18 months. I will be open to opportunities that help me to achieve this and I will work hard to build my business to make this happen. I am focused and excited about achieving my goals.."*

Another really important question, that is essential in this process that deserves its own paragraph is, how will you feel?

How will you feel when you achieve your goals?

Happy, ecstatic, amazed, excited, awesome, wonderful, inspired, proud of myself… the list goes on.

Write down two words that best describe how you will feel when you achieve a specific goal

1.____

2.____

You could also include this in your affirmation. Imagine you have achieved your goals already and speak in the present tense.

For example,

"I am debt free and I feel ________________*"*

How will you feel if you don't?

Miserable, disappointed, frustrated, angry, etc

Write down two words that best describe how you will feel if you DO NOT achieve a specific goal

1.____

2.____

You could also include this in your daily affirmation. It's important to understand what drives you. Some people work best with a positive emotion – the hope, expectation, and reward of that feeling inspires them to action. Others are motivated with a negative emotion. Fear of failure, for some, can be an incredible motivator, but for others creates too much pressure and has the opposite effect.

Your goals must elicit an emotional response from you. They must be connected with emotion. I call them E-SMART goals. They must be Specific, Measurable, Achievable, Realistic and be Time specific as the well-known acronym teaches but, most importantly, they must be connected with your E-motion. It is your emotion that drives you to take the action or execute the plan to get your goal.

Have you ever been in a situation where you saw or heard something and got excited about it, went home, and shared it with someone else, expecting them to be as excited as you? They weren't. In fact, quite the opposite. They were negative, judgemental, and condescending. They told you, it will never work for you, or they know someone who did something similar, and it didn't work for them. Or it's a scheme or a scam! Etc.

THE LION DOES NOT CONCERN HIMSELF WITH THE OPINIONS OF SHEEP

At that point you had a choice to make. You could have either bowed to their opinion and decided not to pursue that particular opportunity, or perhaps you got 'emotional' about it – maybe even angry or frustrated. Maybe you decided not to try after all or, perhaps you got fired up and thought, "I'll show you! I will prove you wrong!"

This is an example of how negative emotions can cause you to take action, which ultimately can lead you to results.

It's important to understand that the people you shared with are not necessarily trying to be negative or trying to stop you achieving goals, although, in some cases, this may be true. Their opinions are often invalid. After all, the lion does not concern himself with the opinions of sheep. Choose to be a lion and don't be afraid to roar.

Sometimes, people – even people close to you – like things to stay the way they are. They like that they earn more money than you, live in a nicer house and drive a nicer car and they don't want that to change.

SMART PEOPLE GET ALL THE FACTS, THEY DON'T FILL IN THE BLANKS WITH ASSUMPTION

Others are simply trying to protect you, albeit from a position of ignorance because they have not seen what you have seen. The best course of action, in my opinion, is, in this situation, is that they take time to get all the facts and as much information as you have so they can make and give you an informed opinion.

Advertising Works!

Advertising is a well-established way that is used to influence behaviour. This could be to buy a particular brand of shampoo, support a specific charity or travel to a particular destination. In all of these, advertising used the power of persuasion to take a specific action.

When you see a TV commercial, even if you are not paying attention, your subconscious remembers and can influence the brand you choose when you are at the supermarket. The best advertising targets your emotion and subconscious mind.

The next step is to create an advertising campaign with you as the target market. Find pictures that represent each of your goals. An image that, when you look at it, inspires an emotion like excitement, or that reminds you what you want and why you want it.

Some people use vision boards or dream boards for this and that's useful, but be careful not to 'focus' on the images on the vision board. The problem with just having a vision board is that too many people stay focused on it. They hope, wish, and pray that the universe will just bring those things into their lives magically through the law of attraction.

A VISION BOARD IS FOR INSPIRATION NOT INSTRUCTION

Now, as I've mentioned previously, I am not saying that there is no law of attraction, nor that whatever you believe in, be it God, the Universe etc, cannot provide; I do believe that we have all been given the ability to create wealth. We have been given the tools to be successful in our financial and personal lives. The problem for most people is that they never learn how to use that ability. It's like having a bag of tools and never opening the bag.

Perhaps this is just me, but have you ever used a satnav in your car to plot a route then, whilst on your journey, you notice that you are not travelling the route you expected? You get that sense of being lost and the thought pops into your mind, "Did I put the right address into the satnav?". You zoom out on the map and check that the destination is indeed correct and thankfully, it is, then you feel relief. Now, imagine you stay zoomed out looking at the map, you can see the destination, but you can't see where the next turn is. You have to zoom back in to see the details of the journey. You need to focus on taking the right route to get to the destination.

The vision board is like the 'zoomed out Satnav'. It's to check that you are on track and remind you why you are on the journey in the first place. It is inspiration not instruction. You need to focus on your next steps. Focus on the route and the strategy not the big picture.

CHAPTER FOUR

PLAN-ET HOW

The second cog in the goal getting machine is the strategy or plan cog. This is the 'How' cog.

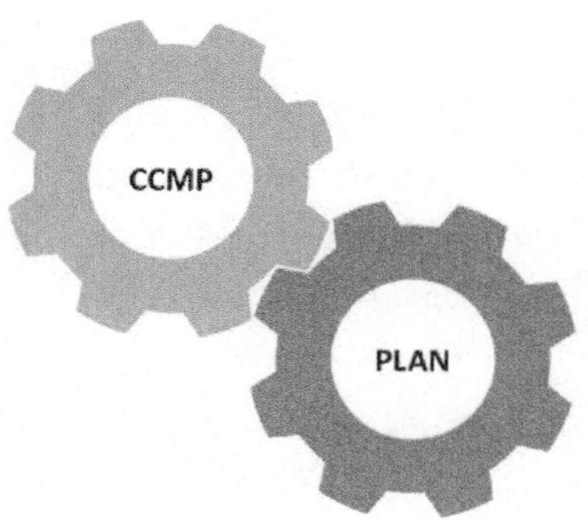

Now you have taken the time to identify WHAT you want you need to figure out HOW to get it.

One of the keys to getting your goals is to recognise that they begin in your conscious mind, but you must programme your subconscious mind to get to work on them for you. Daily affirmations help to programme your subconscious.

Remember earlier, I mentioned that you should write your goals as a paragraph too, not just a list? This is the affirmation that you should read at least twice a day, out loud.

"But Steve, why should I read it out loud", I hear you say.

Because when we read things in our heads we tend to 'skim read' and miss words out. By reading out loud 2 things happen. First, we have to read every word, and secondly, we get to hear it. Faith comes by hearing, so the more you hear your goals the more you believe you can achieve them. This is one way of programming your subconscious mind. An even better way to do this is to record yourself saying these affirmations so that you can visualise them as you listen. More about this later.

Let me give you an example. Have you ever wanted to buy a specific car? You started to do your research on it. You started to talk about it to your friends about it. You may have even visited the dealership to sit in it and get the brochures.

For a short period in your life, it became a priority, you thought about it a lot. Then you started to notice that model of car everywhere. It's like your brain has tuned in to notice that particular car - even on the street where you live - you have never noticed that your neighbour has one until now!
Can you think of an example where this has happened to you? Write it here:

I remember when my son was about 8 years old, he was having trouble going to sleep. Every night I would tell him to settle down and go to sleep and he would tell me, "Daddy I can't sleep!"

I would tell him to try to relax and fall asleep.

"But Daddy, I am trying, and I can't!" he would explain.

I am sure many parents have experienced the same thing. I told him that the reason he can't sleep is because he keeps saying out loud that he can't sleep, and his brain hears it, so it keeps him awake. But not to worry, we just need to reprogramme his brain. A little confused, he agreed, and we started the process.

Every day, once in the morning and once at night before bed, he would repeat after me..

> *"I am awesome at going to sleep. I fall asleep as soon as my head hits the pillow. I have great dreams. When I wake up, I am refreshed and ready for the day ahead. I am awesome at going to sleep."*

Every day we would repeat this together out loud. Guess what happened after 7 days?

Nothing happened...

He still struggled to go to sleep. But we continued our regime, every day, twice a day, out loud and after about 10 days he began to sleep: after 30 days no more sleep issues!

You need to recognise that it takes time to reprogramme your mindset and there are techniques that make it easier to do this.

The reason it worked so effectively with Micah was that he was in a very relaxed state which meant that his Reticular Activator System (RAS) in his brain was open. Therefore, he was more susceptible to suggestion and in essence reprogramming. Also notice it was in the present tense.

The RAS is the part of the brain that regulates the input from most of your senses. It connects the subconscious and conscious minds. When you are intentional in your conscious mind, the RAS causes your subconscious mind to get to work on solving whatever intention is.

Have you ever been in a situation where you had someone's name on the 'tip of your tongue' but couldn't quite recall it, but you just knew that you knew it only to remember it the following day when you didn't need it? This is an example of how your conscious mind gave your subconscious a problem to solve through your RAS. Your subconscious went to work on the problem and came up with the answer.

Being relaxed is one of the keys to reprogramming your mindset effectively. As mentioned in chapter one your RAS is a door or gatekeeper to your subconscious mind.

Imagine the RAS as a door. If the door is closed and you speak to a person through it, the person on the other side of the door may hear and understand some of the words but are unlikely to get the whole message.

If the door is wide open, then effective communication can occur, and the instruction can be fully received and understood. Ultimately it can then be acted upon!

To reprogramme successfully your RAS must be open. So how can you open the door to your subconscious mind to insert positive programmes to change your life?

Just as Micah was in a natural state of relaxation when we reprogrammed his mind to sleep, you need to induce a state of relaxation for your programmes to be effectively inserted into your mind or 'biocomputer'.

I remembered recently how, a few years ago, I used to live in an apartment building with an underground car park. The exit was very narrow with concrete walls, and it was not a straight route to exit so I had to position my car just right, so as not to scrape my bumper or door on the wall. There were many paint marks on the walls where people had not quite judged that distance well.
At the time I was driving an old car, not very nice or reliable, but what I really wanted was a BMW convertible, in dark blue, with a light leather interior. I used to look at videos and review on them online, would stop and look at them in car parks when I came across them, and just imagined that one day, I might be able to get one.

I remember visualising that I was driving my BMW whilst sitting in my old car, as I drove slowly through the narrow car park exit. I used to make the beep, beep, beep, parking sensor noises with my mouth as I got to close to the wall (my car had no sensors), and once I had managed to navigate my way out, I remember pressing an imaginary button in my centre console and visualising the roof coming down and, as I looked up at the roof of my car, I imagined that I could see the buildings towering above me.

Life moved on, and I hadn't got my BMW. In fact, business grew, and income increased, and I ended getting a nicer, newer car. But here's the thing! My subconscious was still working on the problem I gave it. A few years later, one Valentine's Day, we decided we needed a second car and went out to buy one. The second car we saw, can you believe it? Was a dark blue BMW convertible with a cream leather interior! We bought it cash and still have that car today. At the time I didn't think anything of it. It was only a year or so later that I realised what had happened. Without realising it, or subconsciously, I had got the car that I had visualised years earlier.

Sometimes we do the right things without realising, which is good, but what's is better is knowing how you did the right thing so you can repeat it. That's how success and achievement become a habit.

The way to do this is to practice some relaxation techniques. Many people find this a little strange at first as we are part of a 'microwave' culture, but I promise you that the time you take to reprogramme your mind will pay dividends!

One of the techniques I use is to sit in an upright chair, not too comfortable that I will fall asleep, but comfortable enough that I can relax, and play an audio recording which I have recorded of my own voice (this is not entirely necessary as you can have someone else record it for you, but they would not say 'I' but 'you'). I am a firm believer, though, in that you believe you before you believe anyone else, so do try to record it yourself. That way it's you talking to you!

You need to be in a quiet place as any sounds running in the background will be amplified on the recording. If you are anything like me, you may find it annoying. It's also useful to run 'white noise' while you are recording.

Here is an example of how I get into a relaxed state: I play a recording of me saying the following in a slow, calm, almost monotone voice, with plenty of pauses between sentences.

Use this example or create your own:

I take a deep breath, inhaling slowly through my nose and out through my mouth

I take another deep breath, inhaling slowly relaxing my whole body as I do this

I take another long slow deep breath as I feel any tension in my body disappear

I'm beginning to relax

As I breathe in and as I breath out all tension is leaving my body

I'm thinking about the toes on my left foot they are relaxed

I'm thinking about the toes on my right foot they are relaxed

I'm thinking about My left foot... it is relaxed

I'm thinking about My right foot... it is relaxed

I'm thinking about My left ankle... it is relaxed

I'm thinking about My right ankle… it is relaxed

I am continuing to breathe in and out slowly

I'm thinking about My left calf…it is relaxed

I'm thinking about My right calf…it is relaxed

I am continuing to breathe in and out slowly

I breath in and out

The more I breathe in and out the more pleasantly relaxed I become

I'm thinking about My left thigh… it is relaxed

I'm thinking about My right thigh… it is relaxed

Both of my legs are fully relaxed

My entire lower body is relaxed

I'm thinking about My stomach… my stomach muscles are relaxed

The more I breathe in and out the more pleasantly relaxed I become
I'm thinking about left hand and fingers... they are relaxed

I'm thinking about my right hand and fingers... they are relaxed

I'm thinking about left arm... it is relaxed

I'm thinking about right arm... it is relaxed

I'm thinking about My chest... the muscles in my chest are relaxed

I'm thinking about My left shoulder... it is relaxed

I'm thinking about My right shoulder... it is relaxed

The whole of my body is becoming more and more relaxed

I'm thinking about My neck... it is relaxed

All tension has been released

My head is becoming heavy and is relaxed

I'm thinking about The muscles in my face and they are relaxed and so are the muscles around my eyes.. there is no tension.. just relaxation

My eyelids are becoming heavier and heavier

All tension has disappeared

All the parts of my body are in a deep state of relaxation.

I feel completely relaxed and very comfortable.

My whole body is totally relaxed

My mind is open to receive new, positive programming

I am now in a complete state of relaxation

After this, you need to record two or three lines of a goal – headlines – which is followed by 45 seconds of 'white noise'

during which time you visualise, in as much detail and as vividly as possible, the goal you are listening to.
As a beginning, it is worth inserting a new programme into your right brain, to encourage you to regularly relax and affirm your goals.

You could say this:

I have made the definite decision to become a mind power person

I insert the correct programs into my biocomputer for success by listening to audios.

I visualise the outcome twice a day in colour and in detail evoking emotion as I imagine.

After you have added your goals (no more than 5 or 6), each one followed by 45 seconds of 'visualisation time', you need to close the RAS by playing the following:

I am now coming out of the relaxed state and by the end of my count to five, I will be ready for action:

Five, my eyes are open and I am less relaxed.

Four, I feel more alert and awake.

Three, I feel refreshed and empowered and getting excited

Two, I am fully awake and all tiredness has gone.

One, I am now wide awake, fully alert and I feel AWESOME, MOTIVATED and FANTASTIC!

It took years for you to learn how to think like you think now. It doesn't get changed overnight. Be patient and stick with the process and you *will* see the change.

CHAPTER FIVE

THE FIRE OF DESIRE

The third and main cog in the goal getting machine, the cog with the handle attached, is the one that drives the whole machine. It is DESIRE!

It is essential to have a genuine desire to achieve your goals - a WHY. You must connect to your goals with your emotion. They must affect you. A way to test whether you have a real CCMP is that when you imagine that you don't achieve it you feel gutted, disappointed, that you failed, but, when you do achieve it, you will feel awesome, amazing, ecstatic!

If you don't feel emotion or are just pretty neutral, with an attitude of "if I make it, I make it, or if not, so what!" - you are probably not going to make it, so best think of another goal: one that drives and inspires you and elicits an emotion from you. You need a burning desire to drive you to do the activity, to work the plan, to achieve the goal. You must become almost obsessive about achieving your goals.

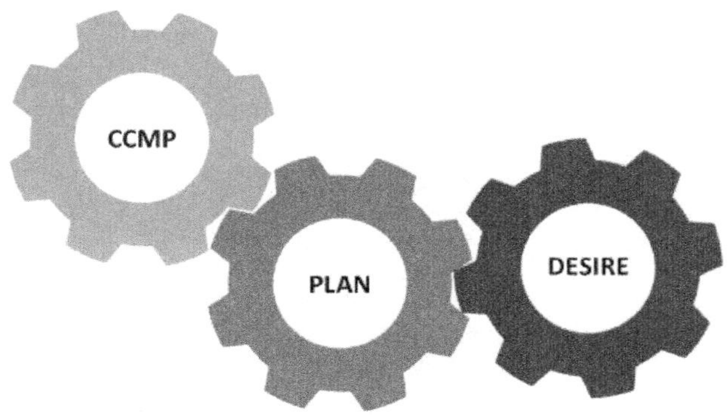

I know that you have at least a spark of desire to change your financial life for the better, that's why you're reading this book. That's a great start! Now you need to fan the flames and add fuel to that spark and build it into a small fire and, by consistent action, building your mindset and belief though good daily habits, turn it into a raging inferno of desire to achieve your goals.

So, in summary, you need to think about your goals. Success starts in the mind. Talk it out loud through affirmations and share with like minded people. This is important. Share with like minded people, not people who will belittle or discourage you from your goals. Share them with people who will encourage and support.

Too many people, even people who you see as friends, will try, and talk you out of your goals because they like it just how it is right now. They don't want change for you or them. Don't let someone who has given up on their dreams or goals or who doesn't have any, talk you out of yours.

DON'T LET SOMEONE WHO HAS GIVEN UP ON THEIR GOALS, TALK YOU OUT OF YOURS

If your goal requires money, which most do, how are you going to make more money? This is another part of the plan. For me, I've been fortunate to be involved in a proven, predictable business which makes it easy to plan my income and financial goals so, finding a business like this can be a big help to you, and one way of achieving your goals.

What does 'future you' and your financial future look like? Use your imagination. Success starts in your mind and is achieved through consistent focused action. These principles are to help you not only change your financial life, but every aspect of your life, as you apply them in all areas.

Many people will tell you that to be financially successful you need to make lots of money! But is that really true? We all know stories about pop stars, actors and celebrities who became multimillionaires but then ended up filing for bankruptcy. According to one study, as many as 70% of lottery winners go broke within 5 years. So, the secret can't be all about how much money you make (or win). It's not what you earn it's what you keep that counts! It's about doing smart things with the money you do get. It's about using financial intelligence.

There are plenty of books on this topic with strategies and concepts, so I don't need to cover specifics here. One book that I do recommend that I find simple and packed with great tips on everything from how interest works, to proper planning your financial life is 'Your Journey to Financial Freedom', published by Jeff Lestz, the CEO of Genistar Ltd., an incredible financial education business, with which I have been associated for many years. If you would like a free copy, drop me an email to mindsetskillset@owbridge.com

This book shares many of the concepts and strategies you need to help you, in a practical way, on your financial journey.

It's important to remember that money is a tool. It's an amplifier. If someone is a good person without money, it's likely they will be a good person who is able to help more people when they do have money. If they are a bad person when broke, can you imagine what type of person they would be when they have wealth? Likely, just an even worse one, who is more arrogant than before.

One simple strategy is to just be aware of what you do spend; have a budget. Start by listing what you spend, where you spend it, what's essential and what isn't. Ideally you should plan to divide up your income into different areas.

For example, one strategy is the the 10-10-10-70 strategy. 10% of your income you give away, to your church, charity or whatever cause is important to you. Wealthy people understand that giving is a good thing.

The second 10% you invest. You put in into a medium to long term investment with a good rate of return and you never touch this money until it has achieved its objective, it has grown to the amount that you need for retirement or whatever you invested for.

The third 10% you save. The first thing you should save for is an emergency fund so that if you have an issue, such as the boiler breaking or the car breaking down, that you have money set aside to dip into to solve these problems.

This helps to stop you getting into debt whenever you have an emergency. And NO, shoes or the latest gadgets on sale do not constitute an emergency! You then live on the remaining 70% of your income.

“But Steve, this is not realistic,” I hear you cry!

“I can’t live on 70% of my income.”

That may be the case right now but instead of focusing on what you can’t do, why not focus on what you can do? Maybe you can start by doing 5-5-5-85, or even 1-1-1-97 but the key is to start to execute a plan. It’s important to develop good habits. As my best friend says, “the person with the most good habits wins”. It is your good habits broken down into daily disciplines that determine your success.

Now, I know what you may be thinking: That this is not realistic for you. That you spend more money each month than you bring in. Maybe you’re living on 110% of your income. Using one credit card to pay off the other and just struggling to make ends meet. If this is the case, then you must change this. There is a simple way to do this. Spend less money and earn more money. Simple right!? But not always easy. Let's look at the first part, spending less.

Complete your budget. There are many free spreadsheets and apps you can download to help you with this. I have always used an excel spreadsheet from one of the free templates on Microsoft excel but find one that's simple for you to use.

How much do you spend on essentials like energy, rent, mortgage, travel, food etc? How much do you spend on nonessentials like movies, luxuries, holidays, food etc? Yes, I mentioned food on both. Food can be a luxury as well as a necessity.

Perhaps you spend money on lunches every day when at work. Maybe it's only £5-10 a day? But even £5 a day, 5 days a week, is £25 a week, £100 a month and, if you're a couple, that's £200 a month on drinks and snacks. Throw in a few takeaways and a few restaurant meals, that's another £1-300 a month on top of your usual food budget. How much could you save each month by making packed lunches and not buying takeaways or dining out?

YOUR DAILY DISCIPLINES DETERMINE YOUR SUCCESS

I remember seeing a client couple once and asking them if they could free up any money in their budget to which the answer was that they couldn't and they felt they were quite thrifty.

I asked a few searching questions and, within 5 minutes we had discovered that they are paying for a movie service that they never have time to watch, apps they never used and, as he was a smoker, he was prepared to at least cut down how much he smoked if it meant they could achieve their goals.

Desire is not the only thing it takes to achieve your financial goals; it also takes DISCIPLINE!

Your current financial situation is a direct result of the choices you have made up to this point. I remember saying this at a seminar I was teaching, and someone said to me,

"But Steve, my wife spends all my money!"

"OK, but you chose to marry her! Still your choice!" I joked.

Imagine a lady called Sarah who is walking through a shopping centre. She sees a pair of black shoes in a shop window and says to herself, "I need new shoes".

She goes into the shop to try them on. Now, Sarah already has 5 pairs of black shoes at home which are perfectly fine. "But not like these ones", she tells herself, "These would go great with my black dress... and they *are* on sale!".

The more she looks at them, tries them on for size, walks in them, the more she convinces herself that she really 'needs' them.

Is it true that she 'needs' them, or that she just 'wants' them? We buy with emotion, but we justify with logic. Advertisers know this which is why adverts are designed to elicit an emotional response.

Why buy a Rolex watch over Timex watch? They both tell the time, but one makes you feel special, important, or successful. The same could be said about handbags and designer clothes.

You may have seen TV commercials for a well known body spray named after a wildcat. The product makes you smell nice but the commercial leads you to believe that you will become irresistible to women and crowds of them will chase you to be with you.

This is why it's important to have an emotional connection with your goals. Let's imagine that Sarah's goal was to become debt free. She needs to imagine how it would feel to become debt free. What would she be able to do with her family if she was debt free and the impact it would make for her.

If she isn't emotionally connected to this goal, then she makes the choice to buy the shoes. If she is really invested in achieving her goals, she doesn't buy them. Every choice we make takes us closer to, or further away, from our goals. By buying the shoes Sarah would slow down her progress to becoming debt free as it would be money she could have spent on paying down her debt. This is where discipline comes in. The clearer your goal, and the more emotionally connected to it you are, the easier it is to make the right choices.

So many people, if asked, 'Why are you in debt?' give a variety of answers. Some of these you may have even used yourself. They say things like:

"The credit cards companies charge me too much interest!"

"The bank sold me an expensive loan."

"I needed a holiday."

"My car broke down and I had to fix it."

"The salesman convinced me to buy a new TV as my old one wasn't up to date."

Did the person to whom the bank sold a loan, *have* to take it? As far as I'm aware, a bank can't force us to borrow money – we *choose* to borrow to get things we *need* but, in reality, things we just *want.*

Did the person with the high interest on a credit card *have* to use the card? If they had savings would they have *needed* to?

Often, our *need* to go into debt is perpetuated by our lack of financial planning, budgeting, lack of savings and a desire to have things that we can't afford today in the hope that we will be able to afford them tomorrow. This is why discipline and the skill of goal setting, having a clear concise mental picture and taking action is vital.

All these may be factual, but they are not actual.

According to some, it has been reported that most people in the UK, are unable to *actually* retire at retirement age. So often, they have no option but to continue working - many times in more menial jobs than those for which they were qualified and employed – just to make ends meet.

The next time you visit a large supermarket or DIY store, take a look at how many senior citizens are working there!

Do you want to make more money?

For most people the answer is yes, the rest are lying or fooling themselves. If you're reading a book called 'Mindset Skillset' with a subtitle of 'Success Secrets for Unlimited Growth' then I doubt you want to learn how to get less money, success or wealth!

You earn money based on the impact that you make. Imagine that McDonalds only had 1 restaurant. They would be limited in how many burgers they could sell, right? But, because they understand the power of distribution and duplication, they have over 38,000 restaurants worldwide.

The impact they make (for better or worse depending on your perspective) means that they make a lot of money. The more people you serve the more money you can make. As Rabbi Daniel Lapin, author of the book "Thou Shalt Prosper" shared with me "money is evidence of serving your fellow man. The more money you make, the more evidence you have." Your impact determines your income.

SOME THINGS ARE FACTUAL BUT THEY ARE NOT ACTUAL!

I once taught this to a group and one man said, "I don't want to make more money, I am not money motivated".

I told the man that I, too, was not 'money motivated' - money did not drive me but the impact I could make using money was more of a motivation for me.

Yes, your impact determines your income, but your income determines your impact. With a lot of money you can impact a lot of lives if you do the right things with it.

I mentioned previously about reducing your outgoings but that's just one step. So how do you increase your income? There are many ways to do this. Let's highlight a few.

You can get a better J.O.B. or 'just over broke', 'jackass of the boss' or 'jump out of bed', as it's been called. To be clear, many people will tell you that having a job is a bad thing but, if it's putting food on yours and your family's table it is a good thing.

It is important to understand, though, that when you have a job, you are simply trading time for money. You agree to sell your 38 or 40 (or even 60) hours a week to a boss for a pre agreed amount of money each month. When you do this, they, essentially, own your time for those hours each week. If you don't believe me, take a look at your job description, and it will often say something like 'any other reasonable task'. This is an employer's way of saying 'if you do all the things we asked you to, in less time than we paid for, that time belongs to us so we can give you other things to do'.

Most people make a 'surviving' in their day job and not a 'living', and certainly not a 'thriving'! Now, don't get me wrong, it is possible to have a good job with a good salary and live within your means, even to reduce your outgoings and invest into your future, as mentioned earlier. It all depends on what your goals are – but, for most people, this is not the case. *They want to thrive not survive.*

***YOUR IMPACT
DETERMINES YOUR INCOME
BUT YOUR INCOME DETERMINES
YOUR IMPACT***

Every year the Times newspaper publishes a magazine of the 1000 richest people in the UK, The Times Rich list. Forbes magazine does the same type of thing. Would you agree that if we did a study on all the people on this list we would find some things that they all have in common?

Of course we would! How many of them do you think are employees? Pretty much none of them - although you could argue that some premier league footballers or sportspeople are employees - are even though many of them make a lot of their money from sponsorship and endorsement deals, in addition to their salary.

On rich lists the majority are business owners! Success leaves clues. If you want to be financially successful you need be a business owner, too. It's been said that if you don't build your own business someone will employ you to build theirs.

It reminds me of a story of a young man who was working for a big company. One day, his boss pulled up in front of the office building in a brand-new Lamborghini. The young man was impressed and, with jaws agape, he stared at his dream car and exclaimed. "Wow! What an amazing car!"

His boss approached him and placed a hand on his shoulder, saying, "Young man. If you work really hard; if you apply yourself over the next twelve months, I can get the new model again next year!"

YOU DON'T BUILD YOUR OWN BUSINESS SOMEONE WILL EMPLOY YOU TO BUILD THEIRS

Far too many bosses or business owners have the misconception that their employees work for them. I once asked a business owner how many people worked for him.

He replied, "50!"

I challenged him, "Really? You have 50 people that work for you?"

"Yes", he answered.

I asked him, "If you didn't pay them, how many of them would still come into the office?"
"Probably none", he replied.

"So, in fact, they don't work for you, or even for the company, they work for money!"

Ask yourself, what, and who, are you working for. If your job or business is not serving you as you serve it, maybe it's time for a change.

What Happens When You Achieve your Goals?

I remember, some time ago, I was speaking to my partner, who was feeling very demotivated in business and was struggling to stayed focussed. As a result, her daily activities had become a chore, where previously they were a joy and exciting.

So, I asked her, “What are your goals?”

“I’ve already achieved all of my goals”, she said. “The house we live in with a big garden, the cars we drive, the holidays we take and the savings we have are what we were dreaming of five years ago, but we have achieved them now.”

I said, “So, what you’re saying is that we set goals, we put a plan together, which we followed, and now we’re living the dreams that we had in real life?”

“Yes!” she exclaimed, the penny beginning to drop in her mind.

“Most people, sadly, never get to live even a few of their dreams and yet, we’re living many of them. In order to stay motivated, we need to research, review and dream about our next goals. All we have done so far is reached one horizon. One horizon reached always reveals another.

We are standing on top of a hill and the view is great, the air is clear but there are mountains to climb and views to be seen and extraordinary experiences to be had. All we need to do is to decide what we want next, then follow the same steps as we did before. That's the beauty of having a goal achieving system – it can be reapplied again and again."

After this, we began to discuss our next goals and over the following weeks and months our goals began to take shape again. We will continue to do so until they, too, are achieved.

I remember sharing with someone that we talked about our goals pretty much every day. When we went out to dinner, we talked about our goals; when we went for a drive, we talked about our goals; at every opportunity we talked – and still talk – about our goals.

Their response was, "Doesn't it get really boring talking about your goals all the time?"

"Why would it be boring talking about the things we are going to do that excite us, that we are passionate about and have an impact on our lives and the lives of those around us. I can't think of another topic that's more exciting. If you rarely think or talk about your goals, you massively reduce your chance of achieving them because they are likely not connected to emotion."

It's essential to meditate on your goals, let them manifest in your mind and your imagination and then talk them out. When you speak your goals, you have to hear your goals and faith and belief are built on hearing. The more we hear something, the more real it becomes in our conscious mind and our subconscious gets to work.

Then, you just have to do it!

Do whatever it takes to get there (legally, of course). As billionaire, Art Williams says, in his famous Just Do It speech, "Do it, and do it and do it and do it until the job gets done!"

THINK IT, TALK IT, DO IT!

If you're not familiar with this speech I highly recommend looking it up on YouTube. It will be 20 minutes well spent.

CHAPTER SIX

AN IDEAL BUSINESS

If you are looking at business opportunities for either additional income or a career change, these are some of the characteristics you may want to look for.

The business that ticks more boxes is, typically, a better opportunity.

Is it a Product or Service That is Needed?

Many people try to make their hobby into a business because it something they are passionate about and love to do. The challenge with this can be that some hobbies are just that – hobbies. They assume that, because they love their product or service, everyone else will. These people can often be seen on the TV shows, such as Dragon's Den or Shark Tank – swiftly followed by those fateful words, “I’m out!”

Market Research is an absolute must if you are thinking about starting a business. How do you know if it’s actually needed, or viable? It’s not enough to ask your friends or read reviews online or look up articles. So often, what’s written online is someone’s opinion based on incorrect information or assumption.

Many reviews of competing businesses are written by people under the guise of service, but the objective is to steer you towards their own competing opportunity. Remember, smart people get *all* the facts. Do your research and make sure you go to the source.

Once you have this knowledge you are now equipped to make an informed decision before investing time and money.

So did it tick the ‘Needed’ box?

Is it a Proven product, service, or system?

An example of a proven business could be a Franchise. The market research has usually been done, a need established and it usually has a proven track record. This is not always the case in a start-up business.

Network Marketing can be another business model to help people build a business or a part time income. Some of these are good, some are great, and some are schemes or scams. It’s essential to do your research, ask questions, assess track record and credentials before getting involved in one of these.

Any Network Marketing opportunity that is not prepared to answer your questions is one to avoid, as is the case in any business opportunity.

So, did it tick the 'Proven' box?

Is it Affordable?

It's important to make sure the business you choose is affordable. So often, people have a business idea, write a business plan, take out a business loan from the bank, thereby starting their business from a position of debt, which often hinders growth. Servicing a loan means diverting funds from areas such as marketing, which grow the business.

One of the challenges with franchises, certainly with more established ones, is that they, typically, require a large, upfront investment for licensing, and there are often costs way beyond the licensing fee, such as acquiring and equipping premises. Many times, there are restrictions on the areas in which you can operate, as you may infringe upon other franchise holders' territories.

One of the benefits of a Network Marketing or similar style business is that there is often a low start-up cost, although, be aware, this is not always the case and most require some sort of monthly commitments to buy products or pay a subscription, which is often how people make much of their income.

So, did it tick the 'Affordable' box?

Is it an Ethical Business?

I would like to think that everyone reading this book is ethical. Integrity is doing the right thing even when no-one is looking. It is not something you should turn on and off like a tap. I know some people have the attitude that I'll be ethical on the weekends but I'm happy to rip people off during the week to make money. I'm sure that's not you. I believe that this is short term thinking.

There is a universal principle, shared across many cultures and religions, of sowing and reaping. Ask yourself what seeds you sow with your actions and, therefore, what harvest you can expect?

So, does it tick the 'Ethical' Box?

What Support is Available to a business owner?

Is there support available in the business? Franchises, as mentioned above, score high in this area as they typically have a proven, predictable, and established system and this duplication is one of the fundamental characteristics of a franchise.

Some Network Marketing companies offer great support, and some offer the exact opposite, requiring you to just get on with it. Make sure you ask questions to find out exactly what support you can expect to receive.

So, does it tick the 'Support' Box?

Does the Business Have Good Growth Potential?

Some people are happy with a small, cottage industry type business, serving a small, select market. Others they have huge ambition and want to build a bigger business.

If you're the latter, assessing the growth potential of a business is essential. We've looked at franchises and one of the challenges can be territory restrictions and the cost of additional franchises, which can potentially limit growth.

So, does this tick the 'Growth Potential' box?

Does the business have Multiple Income Streams?

It's a real advantage for a business to have multiple income streams so that it has the ability to adapt to market conditions. Not all products and services are relevant, or needed, all the time. When looking at an opportunity ask yourself if one product or service was in less demand what would be the others that might be in demand.

SUCCESS LEAVES CLUES

For example, in our business, when the economy is good people have more money, the housing market is buoyant, and people need the services that go with that. When the economy is down, or the country is in recession, people have less money and often need more help or support in other areas. By having services that are needed whether the economy is up or down protects the business, as it's not dependent on only one thing.

So, does it tick the Multiple Income Stream Box?

THE IDEAL BUSINESS 7 POINT CHECKLIST

How many boxes does the business tick? Tick the boxes below to find out.

Is the business…

☐ 1. NEEDED

☐ 2. PROVEN

☐ 3. AFFORDABLE

☐ 4. ETHICAL

☐ 5. SUPPORTED

☐ 6. GROWTH POTENTIAL

☐ 7. MULTIPLE INCOME STREAMS

As you tick these boxes, it's a great idea to make notes on how and why you think that box deserves a tick.

For example:

1. NEEDED. Why is this business needed?

2. PROVEN, how is it proven? What's the track record?

And so on….

I am fortunate to be in one of those rare businesses that tick all of the boxes.

CHAPTER SEVEN

OLD MONEY

As a child I always wondered why my parents weren't rich and some other kids had rich parents. Why could they afford nicer things, better holidays and their parents had bigger houses, nicer cars etc?

At the time, I just thought that it wasn't fair. My Dad was a helicopter pilot in the Army Air Corps. He was a sergeant so was paid a very normal salary. Mum used to do all kinds of things from working in a garage, to a telephone exchange to trying her hand at everything from Tupperware to selling holidays or make-up.

Dad was raised on a farm in times when they didn't have electricity at home and had to share an old tin bath in front of the fire, once a week, with his parents and 2 siblings. He had to go last as he was the youngest and clear the scum from the surface of the water before he got in, as he has told me and my sister many times. How he had to walk 6 miles to school in deep snow when he was only 10 years old. He's tough, my dad. Even today, in his late 70's, he is a tough Yorkshireman, with a great work ethic.

Both Mum and Dad are hard grafters but Mum's the one who loves to learn and is always trying new things so she can learn more. She's where I get my entrepreneurial spirit and creativity in business from. They never had much money, but we never went short.

But why did other kid's parents seem to have more money? I grew to learn that there were a few reasons. In some cases, they actually weren't necessarily richer, they were just smarter with the money they made. Others didn't make more money they just borrowed more and took more credit to fund a lifestyle to "keep up with the jones'" and some just came from money.

I didn't understand how debt worked at the time, so it was the ones who came from money that interested me the most. They seemed to have everything.

If you look at many wealthy people, particularly people who inherited wealth. If you look back into their family history, someone at some point became financially successful. Usually in a business endeavour. It may have been several generations ago but at some point, someone changed the wealth future of that family by making money, creating wealth, and then teaching their future generations to maintain and even grow that wealth.

This got me thinking. How awesome would it be to be able to create wealth, teach our children how to protect it, grow it and build on it. How great would it be to create a legacy that our future generations can look back on us as being the generation that changed the course of our family tree. The great grandfather that became wealthy and affected their generation. Now that, I thought, is a legacy I could be proud of.

I had always liked having nice things, designer clothes, nice cars, and holidays etc. I would only wear designer labels and looked down on people who might shop at ordinary stores or who bought their clothes from Primark.

I wanted people to see me as a successful businessman, someone to be respected and admired. I look back now and ask myself why I was so obsessed with my image and why was I so bothered about what people thought of me. Back then, I was so concerned about maintaining that image, that it didn't matter if I had to go into debt to do it.

I used to love the feeling when I bought expensive clothes with my Platinum American Express card and how important that made me feel. I always looked pretty young for my age so the look of surprise on the shop assistant's face when I bought lots of items and spent thousands without blinking an eye. I was acting like I was a millionaire already, that I had made it already, like I was a somebody.

To maintain this lifestyle I had, what I thought, was a great strategy. I had purchased my first property when I was 20 and it was at a time when house prices just kept going up. I kept getting offered credit cards, so I kept on accepting them. In my mind this was good thing. I thought I must be important if banks keep offering to lend me money. After all, not everyone had gold and platinum cards – how important must I be?

I would max out my cards and then, to my surprise, the lender would offer to increase my limit. Then other card issuers would offer me incentives to balance transfer to their other-even more special - cards. I never cancelled cards - I started a collection. I took great pride in the fact that I had so many cards.

I always remembered an advert on tv where the shop assistant asked the man how he would like to pay, and he pulled out his wallet and a long string of cards unfolded as he said with a confident smile "American Express". I'm not sure why, but that image stuck with me. I always thought how cool and confident he was. He had so many cards to pay from, he must have been successful. I wanted to be like that.

So here was my strategy: max out the cards on expensive dinners out, new furniture, gadgets, TVs, holidays, and shopping sprees. Fill up the cards then sell the property which, of course, by now had increased in value, so I could use the equity to pay off all the cards and do it all again. Genius! I thought. I did this many times and each time, my credit limits would go up as I was always up to date and paying the cards off in full, eventually.

This strategy worked great until property prices didn't go up, they went down! Then things became hard.

I did all the, apparently, 'clever' things like balance transfers, consolidation loans, using MBNA credit card cheques to pay off other credit cards. Literally, robbing Peter to pay Paul, as the saying goes. Then, I got to the point where I had, literally, maxed out all my credit cards. I had a few loans and around 16 cards with limits from £3,000 to £16,000 as well as a £25,000 Barclays Select account (only for special people who qualified, so I was told).

I remember calling a finance company to try to borrow more money, pleading with them that I was a good payer, I had never missed a payment and I always paid everything off eventually. They told me that I simply had too much credit and I had reached my limit. I was devastated. How was I going to get out of debt now? Over the years I had accumulated over £95,000 in personal debt, not including my mortgage. I had dug myself into a big hole and it was *very* dark in there.

I remember just having no money, apart from some coins in my change pot. One day, I went to the shop to buy milk. I took the coppers, the 1 and 2 pence coins - that before I would discard into a pot as they were insignificant - and went to the shop to buy milk.

I remember the feeling of embarrassment when I got the checkout and placed the many coins on the counter as quietly as I could and the cashier did that thing where they count the coins by dragging them off the edge of the counter, making a loud whooshing sound with every coin as it scraped to the edge. Such a different feeling to when I had bought a Cartier watch!

On another occasion, I recall coming home and opening my cupboard to see what I had to eat. I was quickly reminded of the old nursery rhyme about Old Mother Hubbard whose cupboards were bare. Mine were not quite bare but all I ate that night was rice and butter.

Another time, I had to call my parents, who also weren't well off financially, to ask if I could borrow £10 so I could put petrol in my car so I could go to work. My sister drove a 50-mile round trip from their house to mine to give me the money.

I know my situation was not as tough as some people's and I know that you, the reader, may have been in or, are currently going through, some tough times. I hope that my story inspires you and gives you hope that things can change. You can get through it. It's my earnest wish that the stories and strategies read within these pages inspire you to change your financial life and, in turn, your life in general.

I could share many more of my stories of bad decisions, debt related issues, and the feelings of despair and lack of self worth as a man who was unable to provide adequately for his family, but that's for another book. I want this book to be practical for your future and not focused on my past, only learning from it.

WHAT PEOPLE THINK OF ME IS FAR LESS IMPORTANT THAN WHAT I THINK OF MYSELF

So, what are some of the things I have learned from my many past mistakes. I learned that I am special, as I am 'me' and you are you, too. I learned that what people think of me is far less important that what I think of myself. I am a 'somebody' regardless. I don't need designer clothes to look and feel successful. I still like nice clothes and things, but I don't 'need' them.

There's nothing wrong with having credit cards as long as credit cards don't have you and you know how to use them effectively. (I will cover this in another chapter).

Someone asked me recently why I was writing a book. It's for several reasons. Firstly, I created a Change Your Financial Life seminar several years ago and have taught it many times, but it always taught within an hour or 90 minutes and that's just not enough time to share every example and every story. It's never enough time to dig into the content fully so I decided to write this book as an extension of that seminar for people who wanted to take action and get more guidance on how to progress in their financial lives.

It is also my belief that through my own many successes and failures the book can inspire everyone who reads it, whether they have previously ever attended a seminar or not.

Secondly, I get excited about equipping and empowering people to achieve their goals, and this is another way I can do that. As I wrote I realised that this book was about so much more than Changing Your Financial Life but Changing your mindset and skillset and that will in turn, impact your financial life.

Thirdly, and most important to me personally, is that I want to leave a legacy for my future generations. I asked myself, if I was alive in 100 years to coach my sons, their children, and their children and so on - If I was alive through several generations - what wisdom, knowledge and experience would

I want to share with them to help them on their journey through life?

This is a way I can teach my family to not only maintain and grow wealth, but to grow as people and impact those around them for their future generations too. Most of us have an innate desire inside us to be significant. Whether that's in our family or in a wider sense. Ask yourself, what legacy will you leave your family when you finally come to the end of your years on this earth?

Ask yourself.

What Impact do I make now?

What Impact would I like to make?

What would I like to be remembered for by my family?

What would I like to be remembered for by others?

As parents we are taught that we should train our children up in the ways that they should go. Most parents do a pretty good job of loving and caring for their kids, providing them with an academic education through school, putting food on their tables and a giving them a place to sleep. In my opinion, the lessons we teach our children at home and the example we show them by our behaviour and actions are more valuable than any they learn in school.

Good parents encourage, support, and believe in their children. They build them up with words of encouragement and pick them up when they fall down, but how can parents teach lessons they haven't learned themselves, especially in the area of money?

It's not just that we haven't been given financial education but that we have been systematically miseducated about how money works and how to play to win in the money game. We are taught to ask all the wrong questions. For example, when we go for a loan or car finance we ask," How much is the interest rate and the monthly payment?" or sometimes we ask, "What's the APR?". Most people don't even know what APR stands for let alone how to work it out!

So, we are comparing loans and finance based on something which changes depending on many factors such as length of loan, structure of loan etc. Better questions to ask for a real comparison on borrowing would be "How long will it take to pay off?" and "how many pounds will it cost me in interest?" comparing actual monetary cost is a better comparison.

We are sold things like mortgages on our family homes. One of the reasons the banks do this is that they are allowed to lend more money based on the amount of lending they have. Banks have 'lending targets'. They want you to borrow money and proactively market you to do just that.

There is nothing wrong with having a mortgage, but the clue as to its purpose is in the name. MORT means death, which comes from the Latin word Mortus, like in the word mortuary or mortician and GAGE, an old French word, means "pledge".

So, the word 'mortgage' means 'DEATH-PLEDGE'. Not a good marketing name, I know, but it gives you a good clue as to its purpose from the people who created mortgages!! The system of re-mortgaging over and over is designed to keep you in debt for the rest of your life!

MORT-GAGE MEANS DEATH-PLEDGE

Let's assume you took out a mortgage over 25 years at a special rate, maybe a low fixed rate. Three years from now, it's time to re-mortgage as your fixed rate is coming to an end. You now have 22 years left to pay but you haven't paid much capital off in just three years as in the earlier years a higher percentage of the payment is interest rather than capital and perhaps the interest rates have gone up so your payment over 22 years could even be higher than it was previously.

This is when the lender offers for you to take another 25-year term, 'to keep the payments down'. Now, the interest rate clock has been reset and the process starts again. Now, your 25-year mortgage, effectively, just became a 28 year one, then a 31, 34, 37 year and, eventually, you have had a mortgage for long over 25 years and still haven't paid for your house. Interest rates are low at the time of writing this book, but it's widely accepted that they cannot remain this low forever.

Where possible, continue to stick to your original term and even try to overpay your mortgage using debt acceleration strategies if your goal is to pay it off as soon as possible.

This can apply this to investment properties too, if your goal is to pay off your portfolio, but most property investors have interest only mortgages which they just maintain indefinitely continually servicing that potentially 'good debt' and taking a net rental profit from the rent after paying it, and the other running costs each month. I will leave that topic to the property experts to share with you.

CHAPTER EIGHT

WTF!!

What the F? No, it's not what you think. The 'F' stands for something else!

We are discussing changing your financial life, but I believe that changing your mindset and your habits in life in general have a profound impact on your financial life.

Every year in the week between Christmas and New Year we sit down with our kids and plan the year ahead. We talk about what we would like to achieve as a family over the coming year and what we would like to achieve as individuals, and we set goals in different areas.

I learned a long time ago that balance is really important in life. If someone is wildly successful in business but is on their 5th divorce and has no relationship with their kids, is that really success? If someone is wealthy but lives a really unhealthy lifestyle, is overweight and has bad eating habits, is that really success? If someone makes lots of money, works hard all the time and is a huge success in business but doesn't spend quality time with his children, is that really success?

It is possible to be really successful in some areas of your life but not be successful in life in general? Now, please understand that this is a continuous journey, but a balanced life, succeeding in all areas is something to be strived for. So where to start?

We apply something we learned from our mentors, the Fs of a balanced life. Each year we create a mind map of these areas. Family, Faith, Fitness, Finance, Fun, Friends, Firm, For Others and create goals in each area.

I could write a whole book on this subject alone and I'm sure many people have, but in summary this is how we do it in our family. Now, remember at this stage you're setting goals for a balanced life not coming up with the strategy.

It's so easy to start your discussions about what you want and accidentally drift into a discussion of how you are going to do it. Stay on the topic of *'WHAT'* and you can figure out '*HOW*' later. You can't plot a route to a destination without knowing exactly where you want to get to.

Family

What goals do you have for your family? What do you want to do as a family? Where do you want to travel to? In our case, we have a blended family, which means that stepbrothers had to get to know each other better, so one of the goals of our youngest son was “to build a better relationship with my stepbrothers”. These are goals that you can either do as a family, which are related to the growth and strengthening of the family.

You could also add in couple’s goals here too. Perhaps it’s a wedding, a romantic weekend away, to plan more date nights or to just show appreciation of each other more. For everyone it will be different as we are all at different stages in our families and relationships. Talk through these goals with your spouse or partner and your children and get excited by dreaming together.

In our house, we usually show pictures on the big TV as we browse online to share the goals we have and inspire each other.

Faith

Whatever your belief system it’s important to continually develop it, learn more, and grow spiritually. I come from a Christian background, but the principles can be applied to any. For example, perhaps it’s about setting a goal to read more scripture, go to church, mass, synagogue, or other place of worship, more regularly. Maybe it’s to spend more time meditating and connecting with yourself or just learning more about your faith. Most of us believe in something, so set goals to explore that area more.

Fitness

Set some health, wellness, and fitness goals. Are you happy with your weight, body shape, fitness levels etc? If not, then set some goals to make the changes. There are literally millions of books and videos on this topic with whole variety of solutions from eating plans and diets to different types of workouts, equipment and so on. Late night shopping channels are full of them!

The reality is, that you need to make the decision about where you want to be, and then find the system, plan or lifestyle change that works for you. At the time of writing some of this book we had been in lockdown due the COVID19 pandemic and like many people did, I packed on the pounds and my clothes got a little tighter and not going out meant I definitely didn't exercise as much.

Just to be clear - I could have, but I didn't. My weight was a direct consequence of the choices I made in lockdown. In order for me to lose some weight and get back down to a weight I am comfortable with, I needed to motivate myself.

What weight did I want to get to? Why did I want to? What did I need to do to achieve my goal? What was I prepared to do to achieve it? How will I feel when I do achieve it or if I don't? These are the questions I asked myself. Perhaps they will work for you, too.

In my case, although a little bit overweight, I am pretty healthy, so health reasons are not really a motivator for me. For some it will be. You must find a reason that affects you emotionally to drive you to take the action you need. Remember I mentioned earlier about connecting goals with emotion? The same is true here. It can be anything, even something simple.

The challenge for me was that I would love to be slimmer, but I love eating biscuits, cereal, and ice cream more! So, the motivation is just not there. For me it's something simple that drives me. I love going out and dressing relatively smart. I love to wear a nice shirt and blazer even when I'm pretty casual. It sounds silly but I miss doing that and it excites me to think about dressing up again and going out to dinner or a movie on date night.

Now, those blazers didn't fit and pretty soon lockdown will be over. I didn't want to replace my whole wardrobe, plus I couldn't even replace some of the clothes as they are 'one off's' I have that I love wearing. So, I needed to get down to a size which meant I could wear them again.

Sounds silly, right? You might be thinking, Steve, why don't you just go and buy bigger clothes? Sure, I could, but this is what drives me. Find out what it is for you that causes you to be motivated to take action and achieve your health and fitness goals.

Some example: A goal could be to do 100 push ups a day, go to the gym twice a week, cut down on carbs etc. By the way, if your goal is 100 push-ups a day, it's a good idea to start at a much lower number and increase it gradually as you get stronger. Focus on the process and the progress and the results usually take care of themselves.

It's about forming good habits. Maybe, to begin with, you focus on 5 push ups a day, then increase to ten, and so on. If you aim to hit 100 immediately, and can only do 5, it can be demotivating. It's not just about setting goals, but about setting stretchingly realistic goals that take effort, take you out of your comfort zone, but that are not so 'distant' that they feel unachievable.

Finance

We covered this is an earlier chapter so this one should be easy. Start with where you are now financially. If you didn't do the exercise earlier listing your income, savings, and debt this is a good time to go back and do it. Write down where you are now financially and set yourself some goals on where you want to be. Maybe you would like to increase your income by £1,000 a month or save £10,000 in the year, save up for a dream holiday or a deposit for a property.

Fun

What are you going to do for fun this year? Holidays, Weekends away, Salsa lessons, go to the cinema more or perhaps try something new that you have always wanted to do but have never got around to it. Have a think about what you would like to do that will make you smile, laugh and will be fun. Then research it and put it on your goals list.

Friends

Do you spend enough time (or too much) time with your friends? Do you want to spend more? Maybe you spend so much time hanging out socialising with friends that you don't get much work done in your business and therefore don't earn the money you want to earn. They are a distraction.

Perhaps you work hard and spend so much time on your job or business that you never have time for your friends. Neither of these are ‘balance’. For me it was the latter. I can get so focused on achieving my business goals that I don’t make the time to hang out with my best friend. One of my goals a few years ago was to change this and schedule more quality time for friends.

On the topic of friends, sometimes the most well-meaning of friends can be an obstacle to you achieving your goals, financial or otherwise. Not everyone who is your friend acts in your best interests. I have seen so many situations where people have got really excited about the possibility of changing their life by starting a business, earning more money only for them to speak to a friend who has been negative, told them it won’t work for them because they know someone, who heard about a guy that knows someone else and it didn’t work for them!

They literally get talked out of pursuing their dreams and the thing that can change their life! Sometimes your ‘friends’ don’t want you to progress. They like things just the way they are now. They like that they have a better job and income.

Sometimes they don’t have those things either, but are just afraid of losing you if you do ‘make it’. All I am saying is, take a step back and ask yourself, when it comes to finances and the money I need to achieve my goals, if I don’t achieve them will my friend give me all of the money I need? Will they provide for my family if I am no longer here? If the answer is no - they can’t, or they wouldn’t be able to - then don’t let them stop, you

Firm

This is not a fitness goal! Your Firm is the Company you work for or your business. This can be career goals, promotion goals, professional development goals or, if you have a business, then it's business goals. Where do you want your business to grow to this year, income, revenue, turnover, promotions etc.

I set goals in my business every year using the same principles I've shared in this book. We recruit thousands of people and are always looking for good people so I have goals for the number of people that we will recruit and therefore the number that we will offer an opportunity to, to change their lives.

We also set goals for the amount of business we will write with clients and the income we want to make. This helps us to plan our year, our activity and manage our time effectively. For you it may be like this or something as simple as finding a better job or getting a promotion.

For Others

This is about helping other people. I believe that it's an important part of success to give back and to make an impact in people's lives. Whether that is with time, money, or even just kind words. What are the goals you can set for others? These could be something like volunteering at a food bank, or counselling, giving money to a church or charity etc. Whatever it is for you, remember that it's important to sow into the lives of others.

In our family we have a motto that 'whatever time we spend with people (whether it's five minutes or five years) make that time valuable to them'. This could be something simple - from an encouraging conversation or a compliment - to years of mentoring, coaching and support. The important thing is that you add value to their lives.

I challenge you to ask yourself, whose lives do you add value to?

WHATEVER TIME YOU SPEND WITH PEOPLE, MAKE THAT TIME VALUABLE TO THEM

Note that, whilst your setting goals in different areas, many of the areas are connected. For example, a fun holiday goal might be connected to family and finance. A Family goal might be connected to Friends and Fun etc. Each category is not mutually exclusive as they often overlap.

This is a valuable exercise to assess your level of balance now and make a plan to change it.

1. Take a piece of paper and draw a circle.

2. Divide the circle up into 8 equal slices

3. Mark several lines with numbers from 0-10 with zero in the centre of the circle and 10 on the outer ring

4. Label each of the lines with each of the 8 F's. Family, Fitness, Finance, etc.

5. Put a dot on each line scoring yourself out of 10 for each category. For example, if you're really succeeding in business this could be an 8 on Firm but not spending time with your family this could be 4 on the Family Line.

6. Once you have drawn the complete wheel then draw a line connecting each of the dots. This will form a shape.

The goal is to be able to draw as close to a circle as possible for balance and the larger the circle the more successful you are in all areas whilst remaining balanced. This will give you a clear visual representation of how balanced your life is right now.

If you would rather feel free to complete the exercise using the blank diagram here but it's a good idea to draw it out so you really connect with the process, and you can do them for each member of your family or team.

THE WTF WHEEL

You can use this wheel or draw your own.

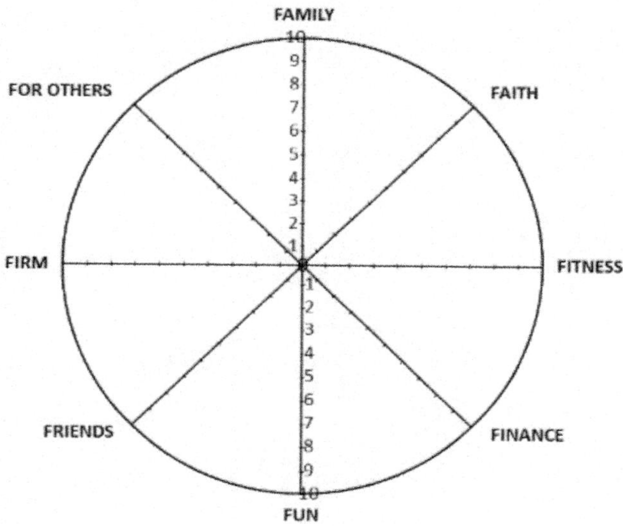

What does your wheel show you?

Example 1: The workaholic

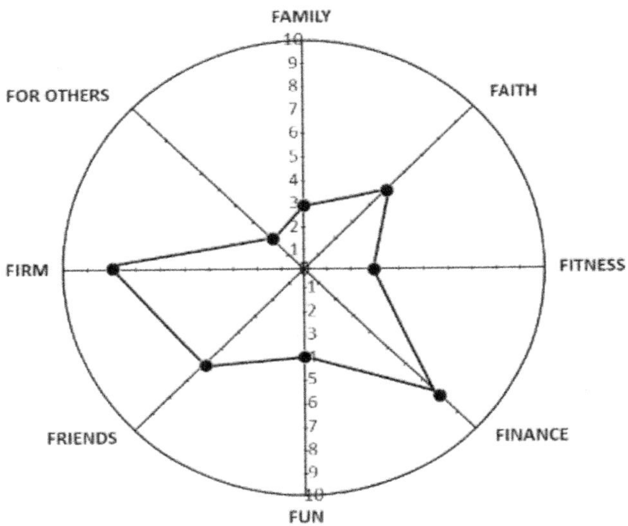

What can you deduce from the shape?

How close is it to a circle which represents a balanced life?

This example shows a person who seems to be doing well in their job or business and making good money, but this could be at the expense of spending time with their family, helping others or even taking care of themselves in the areas of health and fitness. They don't have much fun as they are always working, although they might hang out with friends more than they do their family. These are likely to be friends from work.

Example Two: The Relational

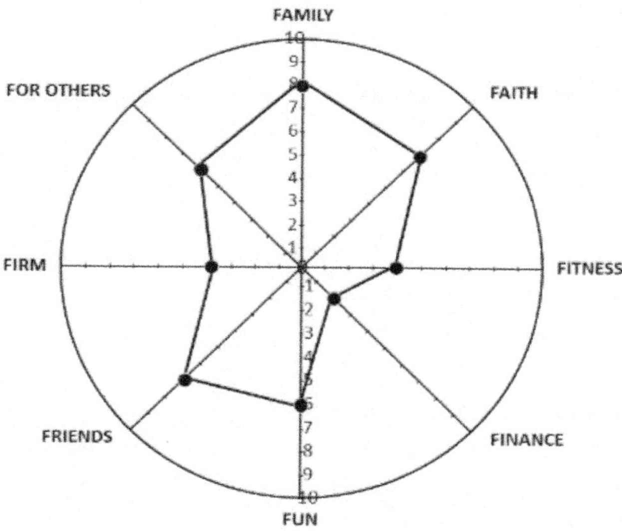

This example shows someone who enjoys life, spends lots of time with friends, family and church and enjoys helping others but they are not doing well at work and don't earn a great income or they don't manage their money well. They are quite likely in debt and by falling short in the areas of finance could actually limit their ability to provide for those people they care about or want to help.

What does the shape that you have drawn say about you? Write it down.

Now ask yourself, what do I need to do to improve in the low scoring areas to bring more balance. Write it down.

Sometimes this means cutting back in areas that you enjoy. For example, the person who made a great income by working too much could review how they manage time, schedule in time with their family or even work a bit less.

There is another 'F' to consider too. That is 'Future'- your legacy - as discussed earlier. This is more of a long-term goal but ask yourself, what legacy will you leave behind? What will you be remembered for? When your days on this earth end, what will you leave behind for your family and others? Wealth or Debt? Blessing or Burden? Many of your goals will also tie into this one, long term.

Imbalanced by Design

Although a balanced life is the goal, there's a big difference between being imbalanced by chance and being imbalanced by design. Most people who live an imbalanced life don't even realise it as it eats up the hours in their weeks and months.

In order to achieve a balanced life, it is sometimes necessary to go through periods of imbalance. For example, if someone has a goal of buying a house within a period of time, they may need to work harder, more hours to make more money to save a deposit.

IN ORDER TO ACHIEVE A BALANCED LIFE, IT IS SOMETIMES NECESSARY TO GO THROUGH PERIODS OF IMBALANCE

During this period other things, such as spending time with friends and family may receive less time. This imbalance should only ever be temporary. It's always wise to try to get 'buy in' from the people who are losing your time for this period.

Equally, when starting a business, it takes more time than when it is up and running like clockwork.

There are three distinct zones when building a business.

Zone One: The Quit Zone

The period when you are investing time and effort but usually for minimal reward. This, for many people, could also be called *The Quit Zone*. For those who can get through the Quit Zone, they enter Zone Two.

Zone Two: The Growth Zone

This is the period when you still work hard but you begin to see an equitable reward for your efforts. It feels like the work is worthwhile. Perseverance, Patience and Focus help you to get through this zone to Zone Three

Zone Three: The Freedom Zone

This is the ultimate goal for many people – to get to a great income, success or results with minimal time and effort. Also known as passive income.

THERE ARE NO VICTORIES WITHOUT BATTLES

There are no short cuts to the Freedom Zone. Part of what you earn on the journey is pride and what you gain is experience. Without these your success will always be tenuous.

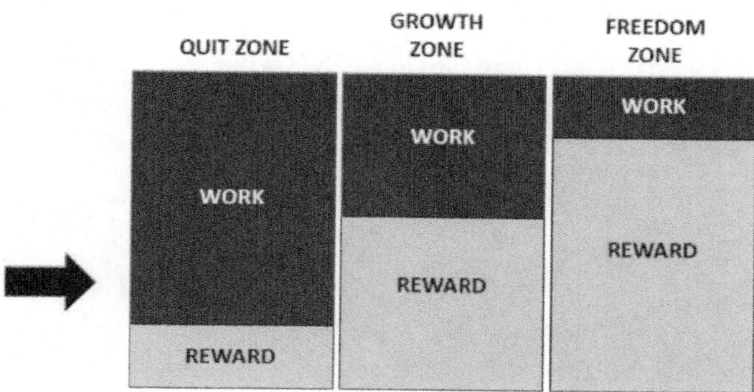

Success in business and in life is rarely achieved without struggle. As one of my mentors has often quoted, "The cleanliness of theory is no match for the mess of reality".

SUCCESS IN BUSINESS AND IN LIFE IS RARELY ACHIEVED WITHOUT STRUGGLE

The theory of growth is a nice, curved line upwards over time. The reality is more like a roller coaster so hang on, hold tight and enjoy the ride. Accept that you will fail sometimes. Failure is not the end of the journey; it is part of it. There are no victories without battles.

CHAPTER NINE

WHAT'S STOPPING YOU?

One day, I asked Micah how he was doing on achieving his goal of completing his homework. Like many kids, he's not a big fan of homework and has a firm belief that schoolwork should remain in school. As I challenged him on his progress, he started to reel off a list of numerous excuses as to why he hadn't completed the task.

"But, Daddy, I didn't have time to finish it!"

"Micah, did you have time to play video games?"

"Um, yeah," he agreed, sheepishly.

"So, if you could find time to play video games and football in the garden, you could have found time for your homework. Right?"

Micah countered that with another excuse, "But, I couldn't find my textbook and I don't know how to do it anyway!"

"What did you do when you couldn't find your textbook? Did you contact your teacher or one of your classmates? You know that if you don't understand something, you can always ask someone to help you."

"I know, Dad. I meant to do it, but I forgot!"

"That's OK, Micah, we all forget things sometimes. What's important is having a way to help you remember so you don't forget again."

Many adults are just like Micah. They still use the same excuses they used when they were kids. Maybe some of those excuses are familiar?

Your excuses are obstacles to goals and an acceleration to failure. Let's look at how you can overcome some of these, so they don't stop you from reaching your potential.

Lack of Time

We all have 168 hours in every week (unless it's our last week!) Some people can never get everything done while others achieve a lot. Some become millionaires or billionaires, and some remain broke. So, lack of time can't be the issue. The issue is time management and/or a lack of understanding of the power of leverage.

In my business, this is one of the most common excuses I hear. One exercise I do with my team, or people I coach, is a time audit to show them how to 'find' more time in their week.

Time is your most precious resource. It is finite. As with all assets, as they become scarcer, they become more valuable. This is also true with time. The older you get, the less time you have and, therefore, the more valuable it becomes.

TIME IS YOUR MOST PRECIOUS RESOURCE

Just as with money, you can spend, invest, or waste it but once it's gone, it's gone. Unlike with money, you can't make more of it.

The lines between spending, investing, and wasting are sometimes blurred so it takes a bit of skill, practice, and discipline to identify which is which.

You 'spend' time doing necessary tasks like making dinner, tidying the house, travelling to work. These are all typically things that must be done. They are not 'wasted time' – unless no-one eats the dinner, for example.

Wasting time is when you get no benefit or 'return' on the time taken. Some would say that watching a movie is wasted time – and, for some people, this may be true. However, for others watching a movie, helping them escape reality for a couple for hours can be a great way to relax, recharge or de-stress. As mentioned earlier, it's about finding a balance.

The following exercise will help you to identify where you can 'find' time that you can invest in pursuits that bring you closer to your goals.

Exercise: Time Audit

1. Write a list of the main things that take up your time every week. For example, sleeping, eating, travel, spending time with family, working, etc

2. Next, work out and list the number of hours you spend each on each of these activities

3. Multiply that number by the number of days in a week that you do these activities

4. Calculate the total number of hours you spend on these activities each week.

5. Subtract this number from 168 hours and write down the answer. You can divide this by seven to illustrate how many hours each day you could invest in something else.

Example:

Activity	Hours per Day	Hours per Week
Sleeping	8	56
Cooking/Eating	2	14
Working	7.5	38
Travel	1	7
Social, friends, exercise etc	2	14
Family, relaxing fun etc	3	21
TOTALS	23.5	150

Total hours in a week	168
Total hours listed	150
TOTAL HOURS AVAILABLE/WK	18
TOTAL HOURS AVAILABLE/DAY	2.6

You may have other activities to list that are regular for you. This is just to show you how to do this for yourself. Once you have completed your audit you will find the hidden hours in your day or week and be able to allocate them to your goals.

Enter your activities here and do your own Time Audit

Activity	Hours per Day	Hours per Week
Sleeping		
Eating		
TOTAL HOURS		

Total hours in a week	168
Total hours listed	
TOTAL HOURS AVAILABLE/WK	
TOTAL HOURS AVAILABLE/DAY	

Most people can find between 14 and 20 hours a week during which they could build a business or spend more time doing the things they want to, just by being more organised and disciplined with their time.

One effective way of determining how to 'spend' or 'invest' the time you've found, is linked to having a Clear Concise Mental Picture. You must ask yourself 'Does this use of my time add value to my life, take me closer to my goals or further away?' If it takes you further away, or slows you down, perhaps it's not a good use of your time.

You also need to be aware of 'Time Stealers' or 'Time Thieves'. No, these are not Aliens from an old black and white Sci-Fi movie. These are people or activities that take your time for things that take you away from your goals.

Have you ever found yourself with too many things to do? You are the kind of person who finds it hard to say "No", you love helping people and sometimes you can take on too much at once? If that sounds like you, I am sure that you would have been victim to Time Stealers too.

So how do you identify a Time Stealer? They are the type of people who ask you the same questions over and over again, never seeming to learn from what you told them already or people who ask you for help with something that they could actually just do themselves, but they are too lazy to make the effort just to give a few examples. I am sure you can think of people in your life like this.

Lack of Resources

As Anthony Robbins said, "It's not a lack of resources but a lack of resourcefulness that stops you." Too many people, like Micah in the story, use a lack of resources as their excuse. In his case a textbook was an excuse to not move forward. He could have found a solution, called a friend, or emailed a teacher, or even researched online.

I come across this often. People can't start to invest in a business as they don't have any capital sometimes even just a few hundred pounds or less is a struggle. They allow that to stop them and yet if you asked them if their car had broken down, on a stormy night on the motorway, and they needed to find a few hundred pounds to get home or get the car towed, in the majority of cases, they would find the money.

So, it not about resources it's about creativity and desire. As the saying goes if you have the want to you can usually find the how to.

IF YOU HAVE THE WANT TO
YOU CAN USUALLY FIND
THE HOW TO

It could be something as simple as borrowing from a friend or family member, who's willing to help you, or perhaps, selling something on eBay or another app.

Most people can make a few hundred pounds just from things they have at home that they don't need but that other people could use.

'One man's rubbish is another man's treasure', as the saying goes.

Be creative and solution oriented. Instead of focusing on what you CAN'T do, why not try focusing on what you CAN do!

Lack of Skills

Micah said he didn't know what to do. He lacked knowledge. I couldn't count how many times I've heard that excuse. "I would do it if I only knew how" or "If I knew more I could make it".

If you lack skills, that's awesome as you know that it's a problem with a definite solution. The solution is to learn. Open your mind and get to work on finding out how. As humans, we have an in-built desire to learn. We often do it subconsciously without even realising. If that's the case, how much more can we learn if we make a conscious effort to up skill ourselves?

Once again, it comes down to our desire to learn, rather than our ability. If you can tap into your desire by connecting goals with emotion, as I shared earlier, it's much easier to learn, as you are motivated to do so.

Having a Clear Concise Mental Picture is the foundation you must build on if you are to succeed in a meaningful way.

Lack of Organisation

"I forgot" – How many times have you said this in your head but made a different excuse out loud? Ironically, this can be an excuse and the truth. If you genuinely forgot, it's ok to say so, especially with an apology attached and, ideally, an alternative solution. But why do people forget? Often. it's not down to a bad memory but a lack of organisational skills or discipline. I recall, in my sales days, an old manager of mine would often tell me “It’s better to have a short pencil than a long memory – write things down”

Making notes, using calendars, diaries, to-do lists or even setting alarms on your phone can all help you to remember. Pretty obvious, really, but organisational tools without discipline can still fail you. I know people who are great at putting things in their organiser but who still allow meetings to run over time, still show up late and still book meetings in when they are already booked.

If you want to achieve your goals, it’s a great idea to work on being more organised and disciplined. Make a decision to work on your time management skills, so you are reminded more and forget less.

CHAPTER TEN

DO YOU MIND?

Many of us have heard the quote "Knowledge is Power" which is originally attributed to Sir Francis Bacon. His actual quote was "Knowledge *itself* is Power" which is more of a definition of knowledge being the "ability to take effective action".

Think about that for a minute: knowledge, just knowing things, gives you the ability to take effective action. Having an ability is like having potential. If it is never fulfilled it is worthless.

One of the biggest tragedies is unfulfilled potential. Equally having knowledge, the ability to take effective action, but never acting on that knowledge is worthless. I have met many very smart but very broke people. They are so smart they have studied for years, have several degrees and doctorates, distinctions, and recognition but they are working in menial jobs, trading time for little money to survive, let alone pay off the massive student loans accumulated to gain all the certificates for their walls.

It's great to know things but the real value in knowing them is in the action you can take using what you know to be effective.

KNOWLEDGE IS POWER, BUT IT'S THE APPLICATION OF THAT KNOWLEDGE THAT LEADS TO SUCCESS

I hope you are getting some nuggets from this book. I hope that you learn some valuable lessons, but I hope more than anything. that you take action on what you learn and apply it to change, not only your financial life, but improve your whole life.

I love the word ACTION. I am known for getting people to shout it out at various seminars and events. For me, it not just a single word but one made up of two others: ACT and ON. Taking action means that you ACT-ON good information, good knowledge and good coaching. It's not just about taking random action.

For many people it's random action that got them into their current situation. Action without thought of consequence often creates more obstacles to be overcome and can lead to failure. It's important to act on good information, then assess possible consequences of the action to determine if it will, indeed, get you the desired results. By doing this you can reduce risk and increase your chances of success making you more efficient because you will make less mistakes from taking the wrong action.

Now you have a choice to make. Let's assess those choices. First, the easiest choice of all: you can choose to keep doing the same things that you've been doing and hope, wish and pray that somehow, something will change. The problem with this choice is that no change means no change.

NO CHANGE MEANS NO CHANGE

This is still a choice but unless you are already succeeding it destined to lead to failure.

One of the keys to success in life and in business is the ability to adapt to changing circumstances and markets. Life doesn't always go your way and is often unfair. Get used to it! That's how life works. If you don't have any battles, you can never have any victories. If you are never stretched, you can never grow. If you are never challenged, you can never learn.

I hope that you act on at least some of the lessons in this book, and it doesn't become just another book that you read one time. It's a good idea to re-read, take notes, and highlight sections that you can come back to periodically and, of course, share it with others.

Printed in Great Britain
by Amazon

70941407R00072